A Tale of Wild Orcas
Granny's Clan

By Dr. Sally Hodson
Illustrated by Ann Jones

Dawn Publications

To Granny and her clan for sharing your lives and stories with us;
To all those who help us learn about and protect wild orcas;
To my family and friends for your love and support. — SH

For Granny, her entire clan and all of the marine life who call the Salish Sea home;
And for my understanding, patient and loving husband, Keith. — AJ

Library of Congress Cataloging-in-Publication Data

Hodson, Sally, 1950-
   Granny's clan : a tale of wild orcas / by Sally Hodson ; illustrated by Ann Jones. -- 1st ed.
      p. cm.
   Summary: "[A 100 year-old orca whale named Granny leads a clan of orcas near the Pacific Northwest in hunting, teaching young whales, and establishing a friendship with humans. Back matter expands on orca life, including their language, echolocation abilities, and family relations]"--Provided by publisher.
   ISBN 978-1-58469-171-6 (hardback) -- ISBN 978-1-58469-172-3 (pbk.) 1. Killer whale--Behavior--Juvenile literature. I. Jones, Ann, 1945- ill. II. Title.
   QL737.C432H63 2012
   599.53'6--dc23

                              2011049431

Book design and production by Patty Arnold, *Menagerie Design & Publishing*
Manufactured by Regent Publishing Services, Hong Kong,
Printed May, 2012, in ShenZhen, Guangdong, China
                    10 9 8 7 6 5 4 3 2 1
First Edition

DAWN PUBLICATIONS

12402 Bitney Springs Road
Nevada City, CA 95959
530-274-7775
nature@dawnpub.com

In cold dark waters, a tiny newborn
struggles to breathe.
Little One, I am here to help.

Granny slips
beneath her littlest
great-grandchild.
With a gentle push,
she lifts him to the surface.
The baby opens his blowhole and
takes his first breath.
A new life begins. An old life continues.

Granny guides the baby to his mother, Samish.
At his mother's side, the baby floats.
They breathe and swim as one.
Granny calls the family to welcome the newborn.
Suttles meets her baby brother. Mako greets his baby cousin.
Near Granny rises the huge wavy fin of her son, Ruffles.

One by one, each of the family surfaces to breathe.
WHOOSH! WHOOSH! WHOOSH!
Loud blasts of air and mist explode
from each blowhole.

Voices of the family
surround the little one
with songs of the orca clan.
Mothers and grandmothers, daughters and
sons, brothers and sisters, uncles and aunties, grandsons
and granddaughters gather to celebrate.

The family travels on.
They dive together.
They rise together.
They breathe together.
They call to each other to keep the family together.
They search for salmon to fill their hungry bellies.
Without salmon, Granny's family cannot live.

For a hundred summers and a hundred winters,
the sea shared her secrets with Granny.
Granny knows where salmon swim when tides
change, or when winds shift, or waters warm,
or winter storms blow.
With Granny in the lead, the family spreads out to hunt.

They swim through ribbons of dancing brown kelp,
among seals searching for rockfish,
near an octopus clutching a crab,
above sea stars stretched over rocks,
close to pelicans diving for fish snacks,
under jellyfish drifting with tides.

They swim past herons stalking on stick legs,
beside sea otters dining on urchins,
over hermit crabs hiding
in seashells,
around sea birds surfing
on breakers,
beneath bald eagles
soaring with winds,
by a humpback
whale playing
in waves.

Each of the family sends out
  beams of sonar clicks.
  CLICK-CLICK-CLICK!
They listen as their sounds bounce off
  rocks, fish, and sea life.
  ECHO-ECHO-ECHO!
The echœs return as "pictures" made of sounds.
In darkness, they "see" how big, far, fast, and what shape.
Shark to the right! Squid to the left! Salmon ahead!
With a burst of speed, they overtake the salmon.
Calls to each other flow back and forth.
Tail flukes slap the sea with thunder.
Swirls of silver salmon flee. Empty orca bellies fill.

At the edge of the hunt, Samish watches.
Her rich milk feeds the newborn at her side.
Ruffles catches a fish that tries to hide in kelp.
To Samish he offers a gift of salmon.

A call from Granny brings young Suttles and Mako to her.
Both want to learn to be great hunters of salmon.
With Granny's help, they learn to see outside and inside
  of shapes all around them.
They scan swift currents for echoes of salmon.
They learn the sounds of each salmon clan,
  of Sockeye and Coho, of Chum and Chinook.

A salmon darts out from the safety of the rocks.
Who will be first to catch it?
In a great rush, Suttles dashes after the fish.
But the shimmering salmon
slides out of her grasp,
into the waiting jaws of Mako.
Bitten in two, the fish is shared
by the young hunters.

Graceful sailboats groan.
Swift speedboats whine.
Stout ferries clang.
Busy fishing boats chug.
Huge tankers rumble.
Noise drowns out the family's calls to each other.

Toward the family, many boats hurry.
Louder they howl. Faster they rush.
Suttles and Mako still play in the waves.
A speedboat races toward them.
To the left it zigs.
To the right it zags.

Closer and closer, the speedboat zooms.
Propeller blades scream of danger.
DIVE! DIVE!

When they hear the family's warning,
  the cousins vanish beneath the waves.
With a roar, the speedboat leaps over them.
A boat with a flag reaches the speedboat and guides it away.
The other boats slow down and quiet their engines.
Suttles and Mako swim close to Granny's side.

Around them hover boats filled with people watching.
The cousins swim with Granny through the maze of boats.
Granny spyhops. Mako spins a cartwheel. Suttles flips a headstand.
The people laugh and clap, whistle and shout.
The children wave their arms at Suttles and Mako.
The cousins wave their fins at the children.

The family seeks rest in a quiet cove.
They gather close together and drift with the waves.
Soft calls flow from one to another.
They doze. They dream.

They remember to breathe.

BOOM! CRASH! SPLAT!
Noise from loud splashes awakens the family.
Mako and Suttles burst from the water, not ready to nap!
Each tries to jump higher, faster, farther.

Granny calls the noisy players to join her
beneath the waves they created.
Far below the sleeping family, Granny teaches
the young ones songs of the orca clan.
As Granny's lullaby ends, the singers
return to quiet rest with the family.

When the family awakens, Granny sings
the clan song of coming together.
Through miles of deep water canyons, Granny's powerful voice
travels to find the other clan families.

From near and far,
each family answers
the Eldest Clan Grandmother
with their own family call.
We are coming.

All the clan families, mothers and grandmothers, daughters and sons,
brothers and sisters, uncles and aunties, grandsons
and granddaughters come together again.
A great SUPERPOD gathers!
They greet old friends. They welcome new babies.
They remember lost ones. They celebrate togetherness.

Sounds of play fill the air and water.
They mingle and touch, tumble and roll, spyhop and somersault.
Fins splash. Tails slap. Bellies flop.
Upside-down tails wave in the wind.
Mako wraps kelp around his tail flukes and fins.
Suttles balances a fat salmon on her head.

With a flick of her tail, Granny slides beneath the waves.
Deeper and deeper into darkness she dives.
When she reaches sea bottom, she streaks toward the light.
Water explodes beneath her as she leaps from the sea.
When she can fly no higher, she spins, twirls, and returns to the sea.

Water and wind bring distant voices to Granny.
Not songs of other orca clans hunting for seals.
Not songs of porpoises fishing for herring.
Not songs of salmon searching for home.
Granny knows these other voices that call.

Standing on the rocky shoreline, people of all ages
    sing to honor the orcas.
Swimming along the rocky shoreline, orcas of all ages
    sing their songs to the people.
With Suttles, Mako, and the family beside her,
    Granny sings songs of her orca clan.

Voices from the sea mingle in harmony with voices from the land.
To people and orcas, the gift of friendship returns.
No longer do they fear one another.
Now they sing songs together and share the seas.

MEET THE FAMILY Granny, Suttles, Mako, and their family are real wild orcas who live in the seas of the Pacific Northwest. Scientists believe that Granny is about 100 years old. She is a great-grandmother and knows many important things to help her family survive. Like grandmothers everywhere, she babysits, teaches and plays with her grandkids. Granny's *clan* is a group of three related families that travel together and share the same language. Each of these family groups is called a *pod*. A pod is a big extended family of many generations led by the oldest female. If you are an orca in Granny's clan, you live your entire life with your mother's family. Orca families are very close. They help each other and share food. They have never been seen fighting with each other. There are many other orca clans in the ocean. Each is very different, with different traditions, diet, and language. Some eat only mammals such as dolphins, seals, and whales. Seeing this, early sailors called them "whale killers," which is how orcas also got the name "killer whales."

Grannys' dorsal fin

Ruffles' dorsal fin

WHO'S WHO? For almost forty years, scientists have observed and photographed all the members of Granny's clan. Just like people, each orca looks a little different. If you are an orca, you have your own "orca fingerprint." The shape and size of your *dorsal fin*, any nicks or scratches, and your gray *saddle patch* are all distinctive to you. Using these clues, scientists have identified all the orcas in Granny's clan. Each orca has been given a three-part orca ID: a ***letter*** (J, K, or L) that tells your family pod, an individual ***number***, and a special ***name***. Granny is J-2. Her son Ruffles is J-1. Her great-granddaughter Suttles is J-40. Mako is J-39.

LITTLE ONES If you are a newborn orca, you must swim to the surface to take your first breath. Your mother, aunt or grandmother stays nearby to help. For several months, you swim close to your mother's side. You drink thick, fatty milk that your mother squirts into your mouth. If the mother of a young orca dies, the family helps to care for the orphan. Mako (J-39) lost his mother when he was five years old. His older brother and sister and the rest of his pod adopted him. Granny and his family give him lots of attention.

BLOWHOLES AND BLUBBER If you are an orca, you breathe air and swim in a cold sea. To stay warm, you wear a thick layer of fat called *blubber*. Your smooth rubbery skin helps you glide easily through water. Instead of a nose, you breathe through a *blowhole* on top of your head. When you surface to breathe, you open and close your blowhole. You exhale and inhale with a loud WHOOSH!

SIZES, SHAPES AND SENSES An adult male orca in Granny's clan is about 23 feet and weighs 9,000 lbs. An adult female is about 19 feet and weighs 7,000 lbs. A newborn is about 7 feet and weighs 300 lbs. If you are an orca, your body is sleek and streamlined like a submarine. Instead of legs, you have powerful *tail flukes* to help you swim far and fast. Instead of arms, you have paddle-shaped *pectoral fins* to help you turn, steer and touch your family. Your *dorsal fin* helps you keep your balance. A male's dorsal fin grows to 6 feet tall, while a female's dorsal is smaller and curved. You have excellent vision and hearing above and under water, but you can't smell.

ECHOES SHOW THE WAY In a deep, dark underwater world, how do you find your way, catch food and stay close to your family? SOUNDS! Sounds travel four times faster in water than in air. Deep sounds made by some species of whales can even travel across an ocean. If you are an orca, you have a special ability called *echolocation*. From your forehead, you send out beams of high-speed, high-pitched sonar clicks. When your clicks hit an object, sound echoes return back to you. These echoes create sound pictures that show you shape, size, speed, distance and location.

ALWAYS ON THE MOVE If you are an orca, you are a world-class water athlete! You can dive hundreds of feet deep, but you spend most of your time closer to the surface. You usually travel at 4-5 mph, but can swim 30 mph for a short time. You surface every 3 to 4 minutes to breathe, but you can hold your breath for 10 minutes. With your family, you travel 75 to 100 miles each day. Several times a day, your family stops to rest. Everyone lines up close together and swims very slowly, rising every few minutes to breathe. Unlike humans who breathe automatically, you must remember to breathe, so you don't sleep too deeply. You nap with half your brain resting at a time.

WHAT'S FOR DINNER? Killer whales live in all the world's oceans and eat many different kinds of food, such as fish, stingrays, sharks, seals and whales. Different groups of orcas specialize in hunting different kinds of prey. If you are one of Granny's clan, you only hunt fish. And not just any fish. For thousands of years, your family has specialized in hunting salmon and that knowledge is passed on to you. Each of your family needs to eat 100-300 pounds of salmon each day. Your family's favorite is chinook salmon, because they are big, fatty fish. Your family works as a team to find and hunt salmon.

Spyhopping

ORCA SCHOOL
Orcas are the biggest of the dolphin family. If you are an orca, you are very smart and learn quickly. Orca school is always in session. Older family members are your teachers. You learn how to use *echolocation* to "see" underwater. *Is that a rock, a fish or Mom?* You practice your salmon detection and hunting skills. You spend time breaching, spy hopping, diving and tail slapping. Your playmates are your brothers, sisters and cousins. When it's time for "orca recess," you can play chase, wear kelp, or carry a salmon on your head.

Breaching

CAN YOU SPEAK ORCA?
If you are an orca in Granny's clan, you use a language of calls and whistles to communicate. Each family makes their calls with a different "accent" called a *dialect*. Your calls help identify you (like orca "caller ID"), share information and keep the family together.

Tail Slapping

Some calls sound like squeals, squawks, squeaky doors, chirping birds, honking horns and mewing kittens.

SUPER PARTY
Sometimes all the families in Granny's clan gather together for a big "orca party" called a *superpod*. They greet each other and communicate with calls and whistles. During a superpod, orcas visit all their friends and relatives, play with high energy and have lots of fun.

PEOPLE AND ORCAS
Native American tribes respected the killer whale's strength, intelligence and devotion to family. However, during her long life Granny has seen members of her family shot by people, captured for marine parks and chased or injured by boats. Now people come to watch and learn about orcas in the wild. Hundreds of thousands of whale-watchers follow Granny and her clan from boats, shore, and on the internet. Sometimes Granny and Ruffles swim near boats and look at the people watching them. Granny and Ruffles are very famous orcas, thanks to their appearance in the *Free Willy* movies. Once a year, hundreds of people gather at Lime Kiln Whale Watch Park on San Juan Island, Washington, to sing to Granny and her clan. Most years, the orcas appear at the shoreline during the Orca Sing. Their calls can be heard through hydrophones placed in the water.

ORCAS IN DANGER
Granny's clan is protected as an *endangered* species in the United States and Canada. Why are they endangered? Not enough salmon for them to eat. Toxins in the water make them sick. Loud noise from boats and ships interferes with their calls and echolocation.

WHERE'S THE POOP?
To learn how well Granny's clan is doing, scientists collect many kinds of information. Orca scat (poop) is a research treasure that reveals DNA, toxins, nutrition and illness. But how do you find orca poop? A specially trained scat detection dog rides on a boat with scientists and uses his great sense of smell to locate orca scat floating on the water. The orca poop is scooped up and analyzed in the lab. The dog gets a reward – playing with a ball.

HOW TO LEARN MORE
At www.dawnpub.com you can watch videos of Granny and her family and listen to their calls.

For teachers there are downloadable lesson plans and resources for reading, language arts, science, social studies, math, thinking skills, art and careers. Activities include: create a food web, "see" with sounds, use photo ID to identify orcas, perform a reader's theatre play, explore a kelp forest ecosystem, make a story quilt, track an orca pod, stay warm with blubber, play an orca survival game, construct an ocean diorama, design a healthy habitat for orcas, write an orca picture book, interview an orca, "be an orca scientist," trace a salmon's journey home, and calculate how many salmon an orca needs to eat. Objectives are tied to national and state standards.

These websites have lots more information:

American Cetacean Society, www.acsonline.org

Center for Whale Research, www.whaleresearch.com

Ocean Futures Society (Jean-Michel Cousteau), www.oceanfutures.org

OrcaLab www.orcalab.org

Orca Network, www.orcanetwork.org

The Whale Museum, www.whalemuseum.org

A portion of the proceeds from the sale of Granny's Gift will be donated to non-profit organizations that help us learn about and protect wild orcas.

Whether watching whales with kids or teaching a class, Dr. Sally Hodson loves to tell stories. Using the power of story, she hopes to inspire people to care for our planet and the animals who share it. Sally has taught elementary, secondary and special needs students, designed curriculum and trained teachers. She earned her doctoral degree at the University of Colorado, with a focus on environmental education, ecology and animal behavior. While the Executive Director at The Whale Museum, she helped coordinate the successful rescue and release of Springer, a wild orphaned orca. Sally lives on a Pacific Northwest island among cedar forests, bald eagles, and the orcas of Granny's clan. To find lots more about orcas, see her website, www.sallyhodson.com.

Ann Jones taught elementary school for many years, but her love for art found full expression ever since she moved to Orcas Island, Washington, in 1992. She lives there with her husband, three cats, and thousands of honey bees. Her studio is very near to the ocean. She likes to work with soft, colorful pastels, using her hands and fingers to apply the paint—a very tactile experience. She was just getting ready to start painting Granny for this book when she heard the distinctive sound of orcas exhaling. She ran to the shore and there was part of the clan, only about 20 feet away. What an auspicious start! Because individual orcas are identified by their fins, color patches and other markings, Ann made a point of painting the individual IDs so readers can identify the main characters in the story visually. www.annjonesstudio.com.

SOME OTHER NATURE APPRECIATION BOOKS YOU MIGHT LIKE

Salmon Stream beautifully portrays the life of an important animal which survives against staggering odds in one of the most amazing migration stories anywhere.

Over in the Ocean: In a Coral Reef is a delightful, energetic counting and singing introduction to ocean animals, part of a best-selling series that also includes *Over in the Jungle*, *Over in the Arctic*, *Over in the Forest*, and *Over in Australia*. THIS BOOK IS NOW ALSO AVAILABLE AS AN APP.

In the Trees, Honey Bees offers a inside-the-hive view of a wild colony, along with solid information about these remarkable and valuable creatures.

Molly's Organic Farm is based on the true story of homeless cat that found herself in the wondrous world of an organic farm. Seen through Molly's eyes, the reader discovers the interplay of nature that grows wholesome food.

Jo MacDonald Had a Garden and *Jo MacDonald Saw a Pond* are delightful gardener's (and nature-lover's) variations on "Old MacDonald Had a Farm." Jo is Old MacDonald's granddaughter and his farm is such a cool place. E—I—E—I—O!

Going Home: The Mystery of Animal Migration explores animals that migrate "home," often over great distances, by land, sea, and air—a winning combination of verse, factual language, and beautiful illustrations.

Dawn Publications is dedicated to inspiring in children a deeper understanding and appreciation for all life on Earth. You can browse through our titles, download resources for teachers, and order at www.dawnpub.com or call 800-545-7475.